BATS

Bat Magic for Kids

To my children, Cindy, Kate, and Nathan. Thank you for showing me the wonders of our world as seen through the curious eyes of a child. And to my husband, Wayne, for his support. — *Kathryn T. Lundberg*

For a free catalog describing Gareth Stevens Publishing's list of high-quality books and multimedia programs, call 1-800-542-2595 (USA) or 1-800-461-9120 (Canada). Gareth Stevens Publishing's Fax: 414-225-0377.
See our catalog, too, on the World Wide Web: http://gsinc.com

Library of Congress Cataloging-in-Publication Data

Lundberg, Kathryn T., 1957-
    Bat magic for kids / by Kathryn T. Lundberg; photography by
  Merlin D. Tuttle; illustrations by John F. McGee.
      p. cm. — (Animal magic for kids)
    "Based on . . . Bats for kids . . . by Kathryn T. Lundberg"—T.p. verso.
    Summary: Relates information about the life, habits, and natural history of bats.
    Includes index.
    ISBN 0-8368-1628-5 (lib. bdg.)
    1. Bats—Juvenile literature. [1. Bats.] I. Tuttle, Merlin D., ill.
  II. McGee, John F., ill. III. Title. IV. Series.
  QL737.C5L856   1996
  599.4—dc20   96-14760

First published in this edition in
North America in 1996 by
Gareth Stevens Publishing
1555 North RiverCenter Drive, Suite 201
Milwaukee, Wisconsin 53212 USA

Based on the book *Bats for Kids*, text © 1996 by Kathryn T. Lundberg; photographs © 1996 by Merlin D. Tuttle, Bat Conservation Int'l.; with illustrations by John F. McGee. First published in the United States in 1996 by NorthWord Press, Inc., Minocqua, Wisconsin. End matter © 1996 by Gareth Stevens, Inc.

Printed in the United States of America

1 2 3 4 5 6 7 8 9 99 98 97 96

by *Kathryn T. Lundberg*

BATS

Bat Magic for Kids

Gareth Stevens Publishing
MILWAUKEE

Not long ago, on a warm summer evening, the field near our house began to twinkle. It was lightning bug time.

We grabbed our jars and ran toward the glittering specks. When our jars were full, we sat down on the grass in the beam of a pole light. After a while, we took off the lids and watched the lightning bugs fly free out into the night.

For a long time we sat in silence, listening to the sounds of the night and wondering about the mysterious creatures that live in the dark. Suddenly, a small shadow broke away from the blackness and sliced through our circle.

Startled, we looked up at the light, but all that we saw were insects dancing wildly in its glow. We wondered what else was out there. When another shadowy figure darted past, we knew we had been joined by some of the night's most mysterious creatures—bats!

The only true flying mammal, bats fly through the night skies all over the world, except in the coldest of places. They have been around for a long time. Fifty-million-year-old bat fossils have been found in Wyoming, but bats may have been winging through the night for as long as one hundred million years.

There are over 980 species of bats. In fact, they make up one-fourth of all the mammal species in the world.

Free-tailed bats

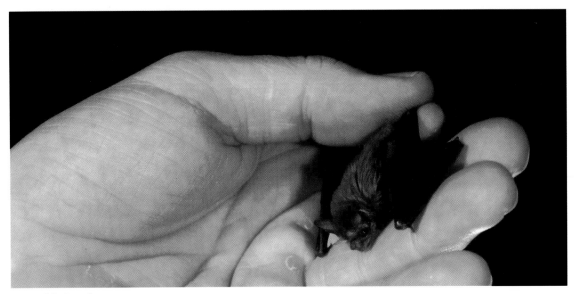

Bumblebee bat

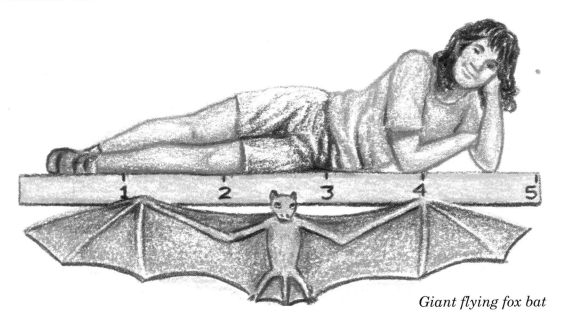

Giant flying fox bat

8

Bats range in size from tiny bumblebee bats to flying fox bats. The wingspan of a giant flying fox can reach 5 feet; taller than most fifth graders. Other flying fox bats have a wingspan up to 16 feet! The western mastiff bat, with a wingspan of around 25 inches, is the largest bat in the United States.

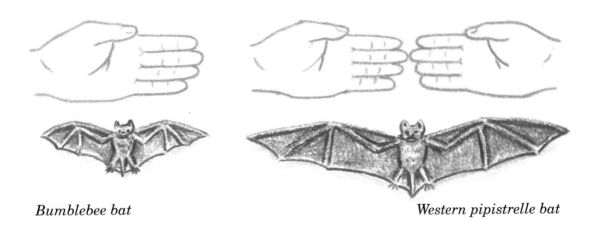

Bumblebee bat   *Western pipistrelle bat*

The western pipistrelle bat, measuring nearly 9 inches from wingtip to wingtip, is the smallest bat found in the United States. The bumblebee bat stretches its wings about 5 inches across, and as its name suggests, its body is about the size of a bee.

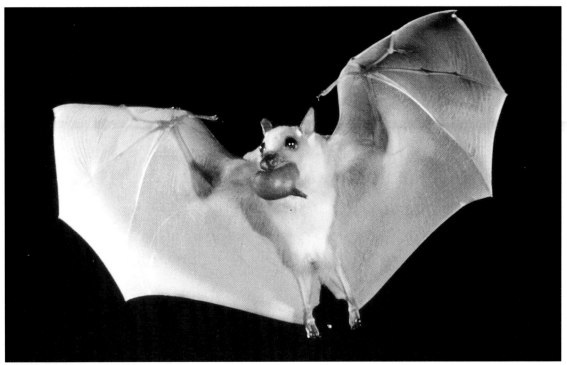

Fruit bat

Bats not only differ in size, but in looks as well. From the wide-eyed face of the fruit bat, to the almost bizarre looking wrinkle-faced bat, and the mouse-like little brown bat. There are bats like the hoary bat of North America, or the ghost-faced bat of the New World tropics, that have small ears. Some, like the spotted and pallid bats of the United States and Mexico, have huge ears. The leaf-nosed bat even looks like it has a third ear, growing on its nose!

Wrinkle-faced bat

We were a little nervous with the bats darting around our heads. These misunderstood creatures fly around in scary stories and live in spooky places, like attics and old houses. Although we were uneasy, we were even more curious. It was exciting to be so close to them.

Bats often live together and roost in groups, or colonies. During the day, they rest and sleep in their roost. At night they fly out searching for food.

Our visitors were little brown bats, which live throughout most of North America. They are brown and furry, weighing less than one-half ounce. If you took two quarters and stacked one on top of the other and held them in your hand, they would weigh about the same as one little brown bat. Their wingspan measures almost 10 inches across.

The big brown bat is also common in North America, and looks a lot like the little brown bat—except that it's bigger.

Little brown bats spend the winter hibernating in dark, quiet places, like caves. Caves are moist and the temperature inside usually stays cool but above freezing, just the way little brown bats like it.

They do not store food in their winter roost to snack on if they wake up. So they must survive the winter on the extra fat they have put on before hibernating.

Although bats in a cave might seem scary, if you were to come upon some of them hibernating, they would be more scared than you. A hibernating bat that is awakened could be in danger of dying. Each time a bat wakes up from hibernation its body temperature rises, burning up precious fat. If awakened too many times it might starve to death.

Little brown bats

Next page: Mexican free-tailed bats

Mexican free-tailed bats like caves too, but they do not hibernate. They migrate from the American Southwest to Mexico and Central America. They roost in caves during the day. Each night at twilight, huge dark clouds of bats—about a million of them!—fly out of the Carlsbad Caverns in New Mexico to search for food. It is such an amazing sight that many people travel there just to watch them.

Honduran white bats

While abandoned buildings are often used as roosting sites, bats call many different places home. From caves to crevices, barns to attics, trees to bamboo stems, bats around the world are very creative in choosing their roosting sites. There are even tent-making bats, like the tiny Honduran white bats of Central America. They roost in groups of 2 to 15, and make tents out of certain plants by biting into the leaves and then folding them along the bite lines.

We were wondering exactly where our little brown bats spent their days, when we remembered the new bat exhibit at the zoo. On display was a simple homemade bat house. We decided we would build one soon, hoping our bats would use it and stay close by, even though the bat expert said it could take a long time for bats to actually move in.

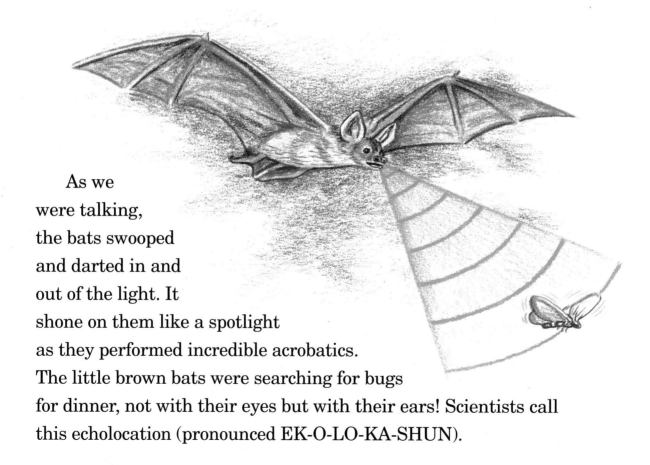

As we were talking, the bats swooped and darted in and out of the light. It shone on them like a spotlight as they performed incredible acrobatics. The little brown bats were searching for bugs for dinner, not with their eyes but with their ears! Scientists call this echolocation (pronounced EK-O-LO-KA-SHUN).

Leaf-nosed bat

Bats make a clicking sound that people can't hear. When the sounds strike something, they bounce back to the bat's large, sensitive ears. Depending on the strength and speed of the echo, the bat can figure out what and where the object is, even in the dark. That means some bats can fly through totally dark caves without bumping into the walls.

Fisherman bat swoops down...

Echolocation is especially useful in finding food, like flying mosquitoes or fish swimming at the surface of the water. A fisherman bat using echolocation can detect a tiny hair sticking out of the water—that's how exact it is!

...grabs its prey and flies off (see next page).

Even though echolocation is a valuable tool, not all bats have that ability. All bats do have the senses of sight, hearing and smell.

Some species, like fruit bats, have special night vision and a strong sense of smell. Each night they follow the sweet aroma of ripened fruit to find their dinner.

Different kinds of fruit are eaten by many different bats. Sometimes the size of the bat influences the type of fruit it eats. The large Malaysian flying fox eats the fruit of the durian tree. The small tropic-dwelling short-faced bat prefers bananas. A favorite fruit of bats all over the world seems to be the fig.

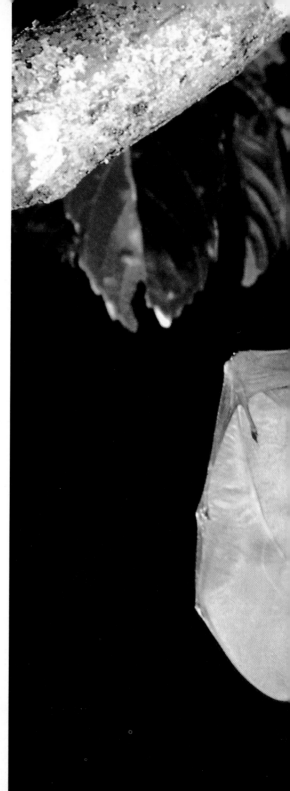

Fruit bat

Suddenly we stopped talking. Something was out there! We could see a large shadowy figure coming toward us through the yard. We all held our breath as it came closer and closer. When it reached our circle, we sighed. It was just Mom. She sat down with us for a while and watched our bats, too.

She told us that some scientists use bat detectors to listen in on bats while they hunt. The detectors have microphones to pick up the high-pitched clicks of the bats. It then changes the clicks into a lower pitch that can be heard through a speaker. The speed of the clicks changes as the bat closes in on its prey, and there is a buzz as it grabs its food. By eavesdropping often enough, scientists have learned the meaning of the different clicks.

Sometimes scientists go into caves to collect bats for more information. They record things like the wingspan and weight measurements. Then they let the bats go.

Bat research

As we watched the bats fly between us and the light, we could almost see through their thin wings. Since bats are mammals, not birds, they have fur instead of feathers. Their wings are actually arms and very long fingers covered with a stretchy skin that is connected to their body. In fact, their scientific name is Chiroptera (KY-ROP-TER-A). It means "hand wing." This wing design is what allows bats to move so quickly. Some can fly as fast as 65 miles per hour!

Sometimes the bats would fly straight at us, and we would dive to the ground. But they always swerved away at the last moment. Maybe that's how the myth that they like to fly into hair got started. The bats were really after the bugs around our heads, not our scalps.

Once a bat flew into my grandma's house. It was very scary—for the bat. It darted around like crazy, but could not find its way out. Finally, grandma opened a window and shut the door to the room. The bat sensed the fresh air coming inside and flew out the open window, safe and sound.

Our hushed voices eventually gave way to excitement and our shrieks and laughter rang out into the shadows. We pretended some of us were bats out hunting and others were moths trying to escape.

Undisturbed, the little brown bats went on with their dinner, devouring hundreds and thousands of pesky bugs. In fact, bats are some of nature's best bug busters. A mother little brown bat can eat more than she weighs in bugs each night. Fortunately for us, her favorite bug dinner is mosquitoes.

Bats that eat fruit or nectar also play an important role in nature. After eating, fruit bats scatter the fruit seeds through their droppings. New plants grow from these seeds. Nectar-eating bats help pollinate plants, like bees do.

Heart-nosed bat

When a bat sticks its head into a flower to reach the nectar, pollen gets on its head and shoulders. The pollen is then carried to the next plant it visits, and this ensures the reproduction of the plant.

The Egyptian fruit bat is one of the main pollinators for the very important African baobab tree, sometimes called "the tree of life" because it is so important to many different animals that use it for food and shelter. If the bats didn't pollinate the tree it might vanish, causing serious problems for other animals that depend on it.

Long-nosed bat

Some bats eat other things besides insects, fruit or nectar. The fisherman bats of Latin America eat meatier meals. Their long legs, big feet and very sharp claws are specially designed for catching fish. Tropical frog-eating bats eat—you guessed it!—frogs.

Alone in the dark, with bats darting all around us, I thought about the legend of Count Dracula. They say he turns into a bat and flies around biting people on the neck. Silly stories like that give bats their bad reputation. Most bats are shy, gentle creatures with very important jobs. In fact, in some places, such as China, the bat is considered a sign of good fortune.

Frog-eating bat

Vampire bat

There are bats, however, that live on the fresh blood of living animals. Vampire bats, found only in Central and South America, drink the blood of large animals like cows, sheep and horses while they are sleeping. The bat's bite is so painless that the animals usually don't even wake up when they are bitten. The bat drinks all it needs, and the animal doesn't miss the blood at all. Vampire bats usually only drink about one tablespoon of blood per day—not very much.

Vampire bats, like other mammals, sometimes have rabies and can infect animals they bite. Most other types of bats rarely have rabies, but it is best never to handle them, or any animal you find in the wild.

Bats also provide a useful resource: their guano (GWAH-NOE), or droppings. Guano is used by people to make fertilizer. Collecting it from caves that have large numbers of bats is called "mining." This could be a smelly job, but not in the stinky way that you might think. The air in bat caves is often filled with ammonia from the animals' waste, which can burn your eyes, nose and throat. It is also dangerous to breathe. Miners, as well as researchers, wear breathing masks to protect themselves while they work inside the caves.

Photographing bats

Our summer night visitors probably first appeared under the pole light in early spring, about the time the mother bats were ready to have their babies, called pups. The female bats form a maternal colony just for mothers and babies.

When a baby bat is ready to be born, the mother will turn right side up, which is really upside down for bats. She holds on to her roost with her thumb claws. As the baby is born, she catches it in a flap of skin stretched between her legs. A mother bat usually has just one baby at a time.

A mother bat leaves her baby in the "nursery" while she goes out to hunt. Depending on the size of the maternal colony, there might be hundreds of babies crowded together. Bat babies, like other mammals, drink milk from their mothers. When the mother bat returns to the roost, she easily finds her baby in the crowded, noisy nursery just by following its call! Some scientists believe the mother also recognizes her baby's unique scent.

Little brown bats grow very quickly. Around 18 days after birth, the young bat is ready to fly. At first, flying is not easy. But learning to fly and hunt early is very important for their survival. Within three weeks the bat pup loses its baby teeth and grows new sharp ones for eating insects. Like their parents, babies must store as much fat as possible before winter hibernation. Healthy bats might live more than 30 years.

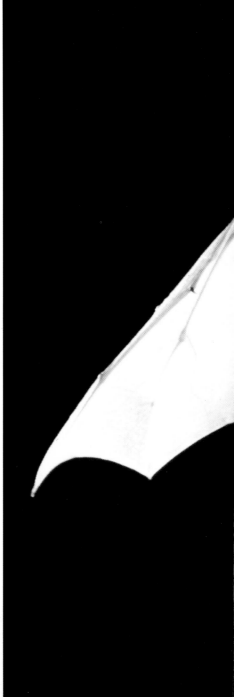

Fruit bats

As we talked and watched, the bats suddenly disappeared. Where were they and why did they go? The dark world around us grew quiet. The night songs stopped and it became very still. Then, the hoot of an owl broke the silence.

Bats are sometimes hunted by predators, including owls. That's probably why our bats flew away—they didn't want to be eaten. In Cuba, snakes such as boa constrictors sometimes eat bats. They catch them as they fly in and out of their roosting caves. Occasionally bats even eat other bats.

Little brown bat

All over the world other large birds of prey eat bats when they have the chance. The birds sometimes gather around caves at dusk to snack on bats as they leave their roost. Small species of bats, such as our little brown bats, have so little meat on them that they are hardly worth the effort.

Even though this sounds dangerous for the bats, predators pose a very small threat to the world's bat population. The real threat comes from things like pesticides, destruction of their habitats, and people. These are reasons to be concerned for the future of bats. Pesticides used to control insects can hurt the bats that feed on them. People also use up habitat for things like logging and housing.

Careless and thoughtless actions by people can also cause problems for bats. Once we were camping with a group of friends, and some of them thought it would be fun to knock down these old, dead trees. Just before it was too late, we discovered that the trees were home to a group of bats. The trees were also shelter for other animals. Fortunately, we left the trees alone. Many people see bats as bad or, at the very least, unimportant. But in some countries, people are so concerned about the future that they have made laws to protect these shy and gentle creatures of the night.

Flying fox bats

Long-nosed bats

GLOSSARY

Chiroptera: The order, or group, of animals that includes bats (page 30).

Colonies: Groups of animals existing together (page 12).

Echolocation: A process by which an animal locates objects using sound waves that are reflected back to the animal (page 20).

Guano: Bat droppings, often used as fertilizer (page 38).

Hibernating: Going through winter in a resting state (page 15).

Maternal colony: A group of mother bats and their young that live closely together (page 39).

Migrate: To move from one area to another, often in search of food (page 18).

Nectar: The sweet liquid produced by a flower that is attractive to insects (page 33).

Pollen: Tiny grains that fertilize female plant cells to produce seeds (page 34).

Predator: An animal that hunts other animals for food (page 42).

Prey: An animal hunted by other animals for food (page 43).

Roost (v): To sleep or rest (page 12).

Species: A group of animals or plants that have similar characteristics (page 6).

ADULT-CHILD INTERACTION QUESTIONS

These are questions designed to encourage young readers to participate in further study and discussion of bats.

1. Are there any threatened or endangered species of bats?

2. What other animals, besides bats, pollinate flowers?

3. Are all bats nocturnal, or active at night?

4. How many mosquitoes can a little brown bat eat in one night?

5. What does a bat house look like? Where should it be placed?

6. How do scientists track the movements and migration of bats?

7. What is sonar? How is it related to bats?

8. What species of bats can be found in your state?

9. What should you do if you find an injured bat?
   If a bat gets into your house?

MORE BOOKS TO READ

Amazing Bats by Frank Greenaway (Knopf)
The Bat by Nina Leen (Holt, Rinehart and Winston)
The Bat in the Cave by Helen Riley (Gareth Stevens)
Bats by Susan Heinrichs Gray (Childrens Press)
Bats in the Dark by John Kaufmann (Crowell)
Bats: Mysterious Flyers of the Night by Dee Stuart (Carolrhoda)
Secrets of the Animal World (series). Bats by Eulalia Garcia
   (Gareth Stevens)
Vampire Bats by Laurence Pringle (Morrow)
The World of Bats by Virginia Harrison (Gareth Stevens)

VIDEOS

Animals That Fly (Phoenix/BFA)
Bats (Bullfrog Films)
Vampire (Coronet)